DEEP TOO

DEEP TOO

Stan Dragland

BookThug
2013

FIRST EDITION

The production of this book was made possible through the generous assistance of The Canada Council for the Arts and The Ontario Arts Council.

Canada Council for the Arts Conseil des Arts du Canada

ONTARIO ARTS COUNCIL CONSEIL DES ARTS DE L'ONTARIO

LIBRARY AND ARCHIVES CANADA CATALOGUING IN PUBLICATION

Dragland, Stan, 1942-, author
Deep too / Stan Dragland. -- First edition.

(Department of critical thought ; no. 8) Includes bibliographical references. Issued in print and electronic formats.
ISBN 978-1-927040-82-9 (pbk.). ISBN 978-1-927040-92-8 (epub).
ISBN 978-1-77166-014-3 (mobi). ISBN 978-1-77166-015-0 (pdf).

I. Title. II. Series: Department of critical thought ; no. 8

PS8557.R275D44 2013 C814'.54 C2013-903521-4
C2013-903522-2

PRINTED IN CANADA

For Robert Kroetsch

Business is war. I go out there, I want to kill the competitors. I want to make their lives miserable. I want to steal their market share. I want them to fear me and I want everyone on my team thinking we're going to win.
– *Kevin O'Leary*

"Fuck a snake right now, if I could get somebody to hold it."
– *Web*

Come
from the other side, from underneath
erasure, chew your way through light toward
different intelligence . . .
– *Jan Zwicky*

1
FOR THE MONEY

Lyle Lovett and his Large Band at Massey Hall, Toronto, nineteen-eighty something. Found my seat, then headed for the washroom to relieve myself, for my greater comfort during the concert, & there was the Men's occupied by women made militant & gone guerilla by the standard unfairness: way more facilities for men than for women. There was a long line of women outside the Women's & another long line of women *inside* the Men's. What to do? I needed a leak, but I was not about to walk up to the urinal, unzip & proceed. Not in front of all those female strangers. Hauling out the equipment is not supposed to be a performance. Especially private, in my opinion, is that waist dip & butt-bob as you haul it back in. So I had two choices. I could suck it up, as they say, suck it up & return to my seat in mild but growing discomfort. Or I could endorse the caper of these high-spirited, grinning ladies, join the queue & wait my turn for the single stall. The decision had to be made instantly, you understand. Telling about it takes a lot longer.

I really wanted a leak.

I joined the ladies.

I had shuffled ahead just a couple of places, when a man's voice behind us blurted, "Jesus Christ!" We all looked around. Nobody. Gone. Seems like *some* men haven't got the stones to join a lineup of ladies in the Men's.

So it's finally my turn. I close the stall door, unzip, take my stance. Outside, I hear a musing, quiet but perfectly clear: "Strange to see the feet pointed in that direction." Then another voice, cautioning: "Yes, but we'd better be quiet or he won't be able." True, there is more than one kind of performance anxiety. Grateful not to be discussed any further, I whiz, flush, exit the stall & head for the door, smiling a complicit smile as I pass the queue.

From: "Lawrence R. Thompson"
To: "Curtis L. Garcia"
Sent: Monday, September 10, 2007 6:08 AM

Womens always whizgiggled at me and even youths did in the civil comfort station! Well, now I smil at them, because I took Me-ga-Dik for 7 months and now my pecker is extremely greater than national.

Michael comes back to the table where I'm waiting with my cue. He's chuckling & shaking his head. "There was this guy at one of the other urinals in there," he says. "'Sure is cold,' the guy said, & I said 'What's cold?' & he said, 'No, no, you're supposed to say & deep too. I know that,' he said, 'because I run the place.'"

The place is The Brass Rack, on Water Street. Michael & I have been playing some pool & enjoying the twelve buck bucket of beer on ice.

"What did you say?"

"I didn't say anything. I just laughed."

I laughed too. For one thing, I was putting myself in Michael's place, baffled but amused.

The other thing was – & what are the chances of this? – I happened to know what the guy was going for. I'd heard it told as a joke in *Sling Blade*, a movie written & directed by Billy Bob Thornton. Billy Bob also plays Karl Childers, the main character, who other people in the movie call retarded. He certainly is slow. Hasn't got much to say to anyone. Keeps mostly to himself after being released from what he calls "the Nervous Hospital," his home for seventeen years after he knifed the man who was raping his mother. Karl was only twelve then, & that's how he read the situation. But then he had to defend himself with the knife when his mother got up & attacked him. She had actually been enjoying herself.

Back in his Arkansas hometown, Karl is offered a job fixing small engines. He hears his new boss tell the joke during lunch at the shop. His co-worker, Scooter, snickers his head off. Karl doesn't seem to be paying attention, but he is.

Now Karl had only just got back home when he was befriended by a young boy, Frank. Frank's easy-going mother, Linda, has this shit of a boyfriend who is making life hell for her, & even worse for the inconvenient son. The evil of it eats at Karl. One night he's in the house when the boyfriend throws a harrowing tantrum, & that gnaws at Karl's vitals. So next morning he comes into the kitchen where Linda is nursing a cup of coffee & says, right out of the blue, "There's these two fellers standing on the bridge, going to the bathroom. One feller says that water is a-cold. The other feller says the water's deep. I believe one feller come from Arkansas. Get it?" Never having heard Karl speak except when spoken to, Linda is amazed. She has no more clue about what he just said than Michael did in the can at The Brass Rack, though she does know he was trying to comfort her. Finally she says, "Well, I be dog!"

There are spots in plenty of conversations when it's your turn to speak & there's really nothing to say, so you just pick up one of those ready-made fillers & drop it into the conversational hole. "Well, I'll be damned!" "You don't say!" "Isn't that a caution!" "You just said a mouthful!" "You ain't just a-whistlin Dixie!" It moves things along. My Newfoundland friends have a compact multi-use expression for that. "Now 'den," they say, with emphasis on the first syllable, meaning "How 'bout that!" or "All righty now, what's next?" That kind of thing.

Now 'den, here is what Karl was going for, he & the owner of The Brass Rack: "Scooter, did I tell you the one about the two old boys pissin' off the bridge? These two old boys hung their peckers off the bridge, one old boy from California, one from Arkansas. Old boy from California says 'Boy, this water's cold.' Old boy from Arkansas says, 'Yeah, and deep too.' Get it?"

My mother had no sense of timing. She murdered every joke she ever told, & she liked to tell jokes. She was no fool, but you need more than smarts to tell a good joke. You need timing. Karl isn't lacking only the timing, though. He's forgetting his boss's "did I tell you the one about." When he got that far, Scooter was already snickering. Linda could have used the intro. Karl is offering only the bones of the joke, then, & he's also too considerate & too delicate to use words like "peckers" & "pissin'" in the company of a woman. Notwithstanding his violent past, he is arguably the moral centre of the story, & it's a filthy shame that goodness fails to prevent his return to "the Nervous Hospital."

& – location, location, location – it should now be clear that there is no scope whatever for any "cold" & "deep" exchange between two fellers pissing side by side at urinals in the St. John's Brass Rack Men's. I guess there'd be no need to mention California & Arkansas in the joke – the old boys could be from Ontario & Newfoundland; one of them could be a b'y – but there has to be a bridge (or a pier) for the fellers to piss off & there has to be a brook (or an ocean) to dip their peckers into. That's how, with hyperextended dipsticks, they get the temperature & the depth.

Graffiti in Croft Street Lane, behind The Green Room, Toronto:

She should hang on my nob

Nob sounds just the same without the k, but it looks funny. That's one thing I like about this. Another thing is that you can't be sure exactly what this dude is saying. Is it, "up yours, girl-friend," or is it, "hang on, Sloopy, Sloopy hang on"?

Is it time to venture beyond the limits of sensitive Karl Childers? Well beyond the bounds of good taste? I'm afraid it is.

> There once was a man from Nantucket
> Whose cock was so long he could suck it.
> And he said with a grin,
> As he wiped off his chin,
> If my ear was a cunt I could fuck it.

Now why include this kind of low-down performance? The rhyme & rhythm are expertly managed, yes, but that's not it. No, what it does is extend our range into the realm of the all-too-human obscene, for which the verse form of the limerick is so very well-suited. But still, why descend so low at all? Thomas Hardy,

"In Tenebris II: "if way to the Better there be, it exacts a full look at the Worst."

& it is the Worst? / Not even. It's verse.
The Worst abides, biding its time.

As for the content, well, this jasper is only fucking himself. There's something to be said for that.

I thought my companion should see the nice green upholstered headrests on the wall above the urinals in Erin's Pub, St. John's, props for the foreheads of patrons who have a drop too much taken & thus welcome a bit of support – very thoughtful &, as far as I know, unique – so in we went for a drink & to size things up. Hardly any customers on the weekday, as usual, & all of those sitting at the bar with their backs to us, so, "C'mon," I said. Up we got, leaving our pints on the table, & over we went. I swept open the door to the Men's.

There was a man pissing at one of the urinals. I had instantly transformed a companion into a voyeur. Me too, I guess. I mean, you should have seen her head snap back, & you should have seen her hightail it out of there. You should have heard me laugh.

So that's that, good idea gone bad. Damn shame. She won't ever be looking in that door again. I had to persuade her out of her coat & back into her seat – finish our beer – & even then there was still only the one of us laughing.

From: "Bonnie L. Villanueva"

To: "Isaiah P. Deleon"

Sent: Wednesday, September 12, 2007 10:57 AM

Dolls always whooped at me and even chaps did in the municipal WC! Well, now I hee-haw at them, because I took ME_G_a_D_IK for 6 months and now my cock is badly largest than average.

When Beth takes her reading out into downtown Toronto, she likes to settle with a latte in a good coffee shop. Decaffeinated, if it's her second of the day. Today's barista in Manic Coffee and Gelato is a touch smarmy, a tall, flirtatious sort of a guy. Beth does inspire flirtation. Once in New York City a suave pedestrian in a sharp suit & toting a briefcase fell into step with her. "You're the most beautiful woman I've seen yet today," he cooed, "Or am likely to see." It was clear to Beth, as they walked along, that he had some sort of assignation in mind. He had a mind for hanky-panky, a nose for nookie. Craved some afternoon delight. Having no such hankering herself, Beth kept cool, kept walking. Politely, but with ardour, she mentioned me. "Lucky man," said the suit, a decent enough loser, sophisticated enough to know when his line & his charms were not cutting it, as he & Beth parted ways.

"Decaf latte!" calls Mister Barista. Beth picks up her cup at the counter, carries it over to the table where her novel is bookmarked. She picks up the book, opens it, begins to read. After a few moments, she reaches for the coffee & sees what Mr. B has prepared for her:

This is not that latte, of course. Beth had no camera with her. No, she found this one by Googling "penis latte." It's wonderful to discover by what inventive methods the wolf currently stalks his prey. Mr. B met with no greater success than his New York packmate, but would have had the subtly compensating satisfaction of sneaking glances at a beautiful woman swallowing a cock of his own design.

Graffiti above the urinal in the Men's at the Ship Inn, 2002, three thought-balloons:

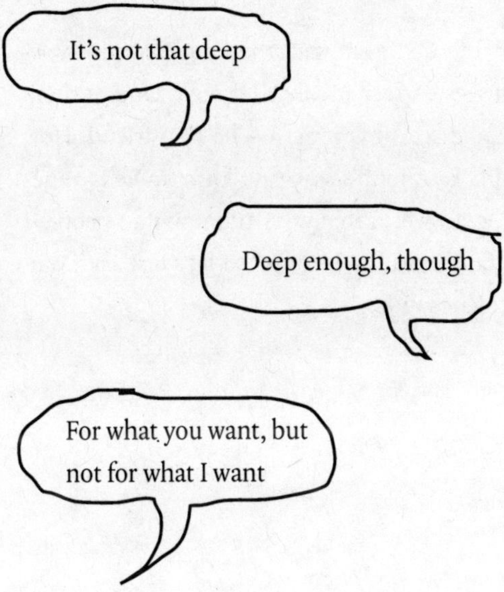

Maybe this started off as a riff on the joke in *Sling Blade*. I hadn't yet seen the film, so I made no connection. I could now, but then I just thought, well, deep & deeper – here's a civilized philosophical dispute, & it meets a much higher literary standard than most material found in a Men's. A lot of that stuff comes from well south of Nantucket.

I chuckled to myself, then rejoined my table-mates & recited what I'd read. One of them confessed to writing it – he & a friend. How tiny is St. John's, anyway, you ask. Well, comes the answer, I'm always running into people I know in vaster Toronto, so let's just say Coincidence Rules.

"They're all the same size," Beth says. I have the feeling that she & her cohort of feminists were counselled to say that to their men. If you're going to consort with males at all, they'd have been warned, be very aware that they're highly sensitive about size. When Beth lived in Montréal, she learned a choice Québécois expression on that very subject: "Grosse Corvette; petite quéquette." *The Alternative Quebécois Dictionary* defines it thus: "To compensate your anatomy (unfavoured by nature) by material show-off." The English is less musical but more succinct: "Big car; little dick."

They aren't really all the same size, not if casual observation in male shower rooms counts for anything, but the long & the short of it is: so what? Why not listen to the women, hear them, & relax. Comparison is foolish, they're saying, & macho competition is tiresome & unnecessary. Forget about Megadik.

With that in mind, let's look at an example: the roostering in *Out of Sight*, a heist movie starring George Clooney & Jennifer Lopez. In one scene, set in Detroit's Kronk Gym, Don Cheadle, as Maurice "Snoopy" Miller, has just cut down one of his sad sack sidekicks for presuming to call him Snoopy – Miller dick is Megadick! – when in comes Jack Foley (Clooney) for a verbal cockfight over who's to be boss of a diamond heist that Snoopy has cut himself in on. The lively one-on-one makes Snoopy nostalgic for the good old days in Glades Correctional Centre, Florida. "It's just like back in the joint," he says with a smile, "Nobody backs down." This is an unusual moment of self-awareness in an often-funny film with a horribly violent ending.

The guns doing all that killing in the last scene are not symbols. They aren't meant to be seen as dicks. There is no invitation anywhere in the film to think "petite quéquette; grosse guerre," so that line of thinking, though very tempting, must be out of order.

Anyway, say an Ontario wife gives her husband a red Corvette for his birthday – I know of an instance – what's going on? I doubt that she means to shrink his quéquette. After all, this is not Québec. In Ontario there is no link whatever between big cars & small dicks, right? (I have heard tell of a Newfoundland-built vehicle called the Drodge Phallus, "the car that's a cock!") No, the gesture *might* mean that the woman wears the pants, but more likely it just says that these folks are not really hurting in the material realm. Unless – unlikely, but I suppose just barely possible – unless the mineis-bigger malady has infected the so-called weaker sex. & of course one wonders what the Joneses are thinking.

There once was a man from Tibet
– And this is the strangest one yet –
Had a member so long,
So pointed and strong,
He could skewer six yaks *en brochette.*

This is more like it, right? The man From Tibet may not be so well-endowed as the old boy from California & the old boy from Arkansas, but he's better hung than the man from Nantucket,. & you can read about him without wincing.

From: "Matilda Y. Christie"
To: "Joseph T. Clinton"
Sent: Monday, September 10 2007 6:18 PM

Ladies always srieked at me and even gentlemens did in the urban toilet! Well, now I whizgiggle at them because I took Me-ga-Di k for 4 months and now my member is hugely preponderant than federal.

I was making a delivery to Webco. This was in London, Ontario. I happened to be wearing that pair of blue pants with zippered pockets. Remember those pants? One of the pockets was a tiny one just above the cuff in the right leg of the pants. I guess the designer thought it would be cool to repeat the zipper motif way down the leg. I could have put some little item in there like a quarter for an emergency phone call, but I never did. I never put anything in that pocket & I had pretty much forgotten it was there until one of the Webco receptionists pointed to it & asked, "What's that zipper?" & I said, not missing a beat, "That's my fly."

I only ever do deadpan, & I could see that she didn't know for sure whether I was joking or serious, & I kept the straight face until I was in the parking lot. Then I let go & laughed myself silly.

There was a young lady of Twickenham
Loved sausages, never got sickenham.
She knelt on the sod
And prayed to her God
To lengthen and strengthen and thickenham.

You remember the cigar that is sometimes just a cigar? Could go for a sausage. I suppose.

2

FOR THE SHOW

There was no Part 2 until my buddy Phil Hall read down to the sausage & said, "I think this has somewhere else to go." No, I thought at first – no, Phil, I'm done. But Phil's sense that I wasn't bugged me. Thanks to his prompt, I began to realize that I was not exacting a full look at The Worst. I was on the surface with Hardy's poem, had not taken it on. The narcissist from Nantucket? Hardly The Worst. Nothing funny about The Worst. To move right along at that point – evasion. Flinching away from a dark opening. Chickenshit. I finally wrote to Phil that I thought I knew where else to go with *Deep Too*, "though going there," I said, "might wreck the piece."

I had found no place in Part 1 for thinking about Ransom Stoddart, Ranse for short, played by Jimmy Stewart in *The Man Who Shot Liberty Valance*. Ranse is a pillar of thoughtfulness *&* sanity in the black/white violent world of gunslingers in this Western. The bully is Valance (Lee Marvin) *&* the good guy is Tom Doniphon (John Wayne). So in this version of the ancient good-evil struggle, there is a mediating third: Ranse is a lawyer, now destitute because Valance hauled him off the Shinbone stage, robbed him & beat him up. Brutally. Ranse is now making ends meet by washing dishes in Erickson's Restaurant. On an especially busy night, he volunteers to carry a meal out into the dining room. He is wearing an apron, so of course any macho shithead would see him as some kind of girly, & Liberty Valance has just swaggered in with his cronies.

Now Valance piles insult onto injury by tripping Ranse as he passes. Ranse hits the floor, the plate goes flying. The Valance sidekick with the perpetual smirk thinks this is rich. He guffaws. But the deprived diner is Tom Doniphon. Remember now, Doniphon is John Wayne. No wonder he rises deliberately, focused but calm, & frees the gun in his holster. "That's my steak, Valance," he says. Valance fingers his own gun, but he's still having fun. He snickers. "Well, you heard him, dude," he says to the still-sprawling Ranse, "pick it up." "I said you, Valance," says Tom. "*You* pick it up." Oh-oh. Looks like somebody got to eat lead.

Now, Ranse is as pissed-off as anybody in that restaurant, or anyone watching the film, but he has his convictions. He knows it would be senseless for one shootist to kill another over a steak. The night will come in this story when even the third man, the amateùr whom Tom has taken to calling Pilgrim, even he will have to walk out into the street, most reluctantly carrying a gun, & meet Liberty Valance face to face. That sets up your dramatic climax. But the scene that most stuck with me from this whole movie was the one in which Ranse Stoddart turns the other cheek. "What's the matter!" he exclaims. "Everybody in this country kill-crazy?" "Here," he says, grabbing the steak off the floor & slapping it onto the plate. That is one filthy steak. Nobody's going to eat that steak, but it has recently come to signify more than just food. "*There*," spits Ranse, "it's picked up!" Which cuts the tension & forestalls the gunplay this time, because nobody had to back down.

The Worst, the Worst. I know it, but I don't want to go there. Rather talk about anything else. Any other kind of palaver, any whatsoever. All night, if necessary.

& you don't want to go there. We need help with this. We need "Instructions for the Third Eye." "There are some who resent the third eye," Margaret Atwood writes. "They would have it removed, if they could. They feel it is a parasite, squatting in the centre of the forehead, feeding on the brain. To them the third eye shows only the worst scenery: the gassed and scorched corpses at the cave-mouth, the gutted babies, the spoor left by generals, and, closer to home, the hearts gone bubonic with jealousy and greed, glinting through the vests and sweaters of anyone at all. Torment, they say and see. The third eye can be merciless, especially when wounded. But someone has to see these things. They exist."

My friend, Doctor Jekyll, was in his cups. He was changing. With the hand not holding his drink he grabbed me by the collar & hauled me up close. "You're pussywhipped," he sneered.

Whatever happened to "henpecked"? Right or wrong, "henpecked" can simply be waved off. But "pussywhipped!" Well there is a range of possible ripostes:

- In kind: Don! C'mere! That's right, over here! Thanks, bud. Just hold these, willya, while I take a few seconds to pussywhip the shit out of numbnuts here!
- Singsong: *Who's* got the *envy!*
- Cool: You may be right, sir, but perhaps we can agree on this point: that is *some pussy!*

& so on. But the surprise meanness tied my tongue. I said nothing. I dropped my gaze to his whisky glass & touched it with one finger, a meaningless gesture. Eventually he let me loose & I just walked away, having, I suppose,proved his point.

Is that it, you ask? The Worst? No, dear reader, it's only a nasty little blip &, jesting aside, you & I know the enlightened way to react: don't. Lump it. File it under Precious Experience of the sort delivered only by your Friends From Hell. Just lightly dispatch it to the proper folder & move on. Sez I to myself. Repeatedly.

Laura Apol was a volunteer worker in Rwanda, recruited to bring her program of life-writing for healing to that tormented country. What she saw there, what she witnessed, well after the hundred days of genocide, was so devastating that she had to seek her own path to healing. She needed to work her own way through what she'd seen by writing poems like this one, about a horrible scene preserved as memorial in the church where it happened:

Holy Mary, Mother of God,
Pray for Us Now and at the Hour of our Death

As if rape were not enough,.
they did it with a spear.
As if a spear were not enough,

they entered her so hard
the point exited her skull.
As if her ruptured skull were not enough,
they did this with her baby
tied to her back,
then nailed the living baby
to her shattered body
with a sharpened stick.
The mother-child skeleton,
a spear run through, remains;
the blessed Virgin, witnessing, remains
untouched.

Mega- : *slang adj.* of enormous size, importance, etc.

Enormous tool. Wipes the smile off your face.

The poem ends with an admission: people like Laura, like me, are privileged. We may choose not to look. If we do, we can still head home to Arkansas or Michigan or Newfoundland

& put what we've seen behind us. Retreat to what Laura elsewhere calls "the amnesia / I call home." But she & I know Atwood is right. Someone has to see things so shocking that, even in the encounter at second- or third-hand most of us want to turn away. "Try not to resist the third eye," she says, "it knows what it's doing. Leave it alone and it will show you that this truth is not the only truth." That much we know, though it bears repeating. And the reward for non-resistance? "One day you will wake up and everything, the stones by the driveway, the brick houses, each brick, each leaf of each tree, your own body, will be glowing from within, lit up, so bright you can hardly look. You will reach out in any direction and you will touch the light itself."

My heart rises to that. It leaps at those living words for a clarity and a faith I haven't achieved & never expect to.

Late in the story of his bad bargain (bought high, sells low), Doctor Faustus cries out, "O I'll leap up to my God. Who pulls me down?" Jeez, he ought to know. He & nobody else signed the deal with Lucifer, late of the light. I did not, but maybe there was some kind of a proxy, because now that I really look at Thomas Hardy's poem I see that, like him, I'm distanced from all the "stout upstanders" who cry "nothing is much the matter." I'm another grounded solitary, cramped in the murk (*tenebris*=darkness) of doubt.

Let him in whose ears the low-voiced Best
  is killed by the clash of the First,
Who holds that if way to the Better there be,
  it exacts a full look at the Worst,

Who feels that delight is a delicate growth,
  cramped by crookedness, custom and fear,
Get him up and be gone as one shaped awry;
  he disturbs the order here.

Yes, a darkness hauls me down. Sometimes down to the rock, bottom. & yet, & yet, my vitals rise to the light. They do. "Everywhere you look," Jan Zwicky writes,

there's beauty, and it's rimed
with death. If you find injustice
you'll find humans, and this means
that if you listen, you'll find love.
The substance of the world is light,
is water: here, clear
even when it's dying; even when the dying
seems unbearable, it runs.

3
TO GET READY

Near the end of George Bowering's novel, *Caprice*, when Spencer, the American bad guy, *&* Caprice, the Québécois heroine, finally meet, they do so up the Deadman River valley in a mountainous British Columbia landscape that is "memory itself. The cliffs along the west wall were inlaid with petrified wood. The shapes of sea creatures hid beneath slabs of stone speckled with jasper and agate." Here, as everywhere, what Loren Eiseley calls "the earth's own book of stone" is a story that precedes us *&* grounds us *&* can be read. What more there is than meets the casual eye in this novel of characters traversing unusually legible terrain may be discovered in the moment late in the book when Caprice's gaze first meets Spencer's. "[H]is face was about ten feet from hers, and it was formed out of a deep hatred that must have been shaped in Tennessee before anyone was born."

The one of these two being naturally, irredeemably, bad, the other having lost herself to the shadow of vengeance for his murder of her brother, Spencer & Caprice have been caught up in an irresistible dance of mutual attraction almost from page one of this serious parody of the western novel. It's no standard fiction, but it's a page-turner anyway, & it's right to read the book fast, just to find out what's going to happen, who's going to prevail. But the deeper story is ancient. In that story the characters are acting at the behest of an irresistible force beyond them. That level of story doesn't jump out. It takes time to grasp. Slow down, pay close attention – good advice for reading anything – & some of the lines that zipped by will stand out in high relief. HATRED THAT MUST HAVE BEEN SHAPED IN TENNESSEE

BEFORE *anyone* WAS BORN. That's before there were people & so before borders, before words. Long before Tennessee had a name.

During the incomprehensible billions of years before organic life appeared on the planet, was hatred already a vein of the patient, abiding rock of ages? Eons before our genesis, before gods were thought of, before any tragic tales of disobedience were invented to make pre-scientific sense of the horrors people get up to, were evil & good already locked in their symbiotic dance? "Once, far north in Canada," says Eiseley, in the age of science, "I came upon a tremendous pile of boulders tossed about like houses in a hurricane. I was dwarfed beside them. They were remnants dropped from the retreating Labradorean ice cap." Finding himself reduced "to miniscule proportions," Eiseley "felt as lost as an insect drifting into a colossal ruin, not alone of earth, but of ages.... Nothing human will compass it save this: we, mankind, arose amidst the wandering of the ice and marched with it. We are in some sense shaped by it, as it has shaped the stones."

Shaped by it. Ill-fashioned. Half-assed. Always, always out of our depth.

Having always been so, love will always be rimed with hate?

Three & we're quits? Third time the charm?

Third means, Third is … a Leaper, a Misfit, a Mother, is Poor Old Harlequin teasing, ripping, banging – *cajoling* enmities into phhhp. Keen eye, tumult of grief & laughter – mediate.

Third space!

Immense, Mama, & it swings.

CITED

John Allemang, "I want to kill the competitors." *The Globe and Mail*, Saturday, September 24, 2011.

Laura Apol, "Holy Mother, Pray for us Now and in the Hour of our Death," *The Back Yards of Heaven*. Unpublished.

Margaret Atwood, "Instructions for the Third Eye," *Murder in the Dark*. Toronto: Coach House, 1983.

George Bowering, *Caprice: a Novel*. Markham, ON: Penguin Canada, 1987.

Loren Eiseley, *All the Strange Hours: The Excavation of a Life.* Illustrations by Emanuel Haller. New York: Charles Scribner's Sons, 1975.

John Ford, Director, *The Man Who Shot Liberty Valance.* Paramount, 1962.

Thomas Hardy, "In Tenebris II." Tim Armstrong, editor, *Selected Poems*. Harlow: Pearson Educational, 2009.

Robert Kroetsch, *Badlands.* Toronto: General, 1976.

Christopher Marlowe, *The Tragical History of Doctor Faustus*. Frederic S. Boas, editor. New York: Gordian Press, 1966.

Steven Soderbergh, director, *Out of Sight.* Universal, 1998.

Billy Bob Thornton, director, *Sling Blade*. Shooting Gallery, 1996.

Jan Zwicky, "The Art of Fugue III," "Practicing Bach." *Forge*. Kentville, NS: Gaspereau, 2011.

THANKS

Laura Apol, Roo Borson, Emma Butler, Michael Crummey, Beth Follett, Pam Frampton, Phil Hall, Mike Hickey, Don McKay (Third Man), Hazel Millar & Jay MillAr, Peggy Mulligan, Dave Sheppard (http://squarewheelstudio.com and www.emmabutler.com), and *The Great Eastern*, Newfoundland's Cultural Magazine.

Megadik started all this. For a while I thought it would all be as funny as those weird e-mails.

Stan Dragland was founder of *Brick* magazine and Brick Books, and is still active with the latter. His books have won the Gabrielle Roy Prize for Canadian literary criticism, the bpNichol Chapbook Award and the Newfoundland and Labrador Rogers Cable Award for non-fiction. His latest is *The Drowned Lands*, a novel.

COLOPHON

Manufactured as the First Edition of *Deep Too* in the Sutumn of 2013 by BookThug. Distributed in Canada by the Literary Press Group: www.lpg.ca. Distributed in the United States by Small Press Distribution: www.spdbooks.org. Shop online at www.bookthug.ca

BOOK
PRODUCTION
WAR ECONOMY
STANDARD

Type + design by Jay MillAr
Copy edited by Ruth Zuchter